The ILLUSTRATED
STATUE of LIBERTY

Nik,

　　Thanks for your support
in steering this book + me
through all the stages, plus
a great job sending it into the
world.　　Barks Barbaria

right: Deck of the S.S. Amsterdam by Frances Benjamin Johnston, 1910

The ILLUSTRATED
STATUE *of* LIBERTY

BRUCE RICE

COTEAU BOOKS
WWW.COTEAUBOOKS.COM

Edited by Don MacKay.
Cover and book design by Duncan Campbell.
Cover image, detail of "Steerage Deck of the S.S. Punnland, 1883"
from the Byron Collection of the Museum of the City of New York
Printed and bound in Canada at Marc Veilleux Imprimeur.

National Library of Canada Cataloguing in Publication

Rice, Bruce
The illustrated Statue of Liberty / Bruce Rice.

Poems.
ISBN 1-55050-268-9

I. Title.
PS8585.I128I44 2003   C811'.54   C2003-911142-3

1   2   3   4   5   6   7   8   9   10

available in Canada and the US from:
Fitzhenry & Whiteside
401-2206 Dewdney Ave.   195 Allstate Parkway
Regina, Saskatchewan   Markham, Ontario
Canada   S4R 1H3   Canada   L3R 4T8

The publisher gratefully acknowledges the financial assistance of the Saskatchewan Arts Board, the Canada Council for the Arts, the Government of Canada through the Book Publishing Industry Development Program (BPIDP), the Government of Saskatchewan, through the Cultural Industries Development Fund, and the City of Regina Arts Commission, for its publishing program.

For Joanne, Keegan, Mira
And grandmothers Pearl and Winnie

CONTENTS

III. LEARN *to* PAINT

IV. ACTS *of* MERCY

The colossal hand comes over the sea in a boat. Inside the crate, it reasons: *The heart is an engine. My body is near, rolling toward some purpose.* Slowly, in darkness

        a voice assembles a mouth
                  and so there is music.

I

MADMEN
I HAVE KNOWN

... it's very subtle and a little embarrassing to me, but I really think there are things nobody would see unless I photograph them.

– Diane Arbus

*The trouble is that I am crazy
and the room drinks me.*

– Anne Sexton, letter

THE MADMEN I HAVE KNOWN

were my companions, the ones
who stared too long into the sun.
Their echolalic music still lurks
where they slept or were hidden away
in a guarded house. This lament
is for you, Don the Rainmaker,
who danced seven years on my corner,
shivering like a reed and
grieving your wife as it rained.
If that isn't Kaddish, what is?

And this is for you, Ronnie No-Coin, burnt-out
denizen of the Venus Cafe. Did you ever get
all those broken TVs and landing lights
wired together, a glimmering nest
of transistors and cathode guns
blinking as you slept in your darkened room?
Did the Strangers return one day as they promised
to get you off this scary planet?

This is for you Leona, locked away so long
even language forgot you. Still, you found
a way: the game with five vowels,
the piano you heard through the floor, sustained
chords ringing; and the neighbour who finally asked
about the garbled noise she heard up the stairs,
sure it was human because she knew the tune,
"You are my sunshine."

Leona, Ronnie, Don, who's singing now?
Prophets you were not, just human fools
who succeeded at that art
we all know best – holding on, holding on.
Old friends, you comfort me.

My Days with Young Christian Players

"...Before Pinel, sixty percent of the mental patients at Bicentre died of disease, suicide or other causes within the first two years of admission."

Someone was late. It was four in the afternoon when Young Christian Players gathered in front of the arching door of the hospital built the year after the Civil War: a hundred and two years later and it still looked the same. My father was hired to "clean the place up." "A bloody Dark Age," he called it. It was like taking an oath, just to hear the words.

He gave us the tour, but not the tour he gave me one year before: beds so close they blocked our way like cast iron spiders – white ones found in a cave when the light falls on them. I could see through rows of rifle-slit windows in one sullen door after another. No one ate there by choice: milky potatoes and salty pork, cooked, boiled, and recooked; the vacant bench on the close-cropped lawn and the dead-end lane to the entrance saying more than the strange, tender shapes of humanity I quickly got used to – old schizophrenics, microcephalics, "mongoloids," others who lurched in place from right to left leg until they were touched on the elbow and gently coaxed away. I still see those pocked walls. They were painted so often they curved in the corners: warehouse green that admitted neither light nor shadow. Every Friday, a dance played by the hospital band – a guitar, piano, a Wilf Carter tune, and life with nothing, absolutely nothing to do.

* * *

Such places have their own gravity and everyone knows it. A bedrock of secrets: lost souls swimming in circles at the bottom of whirlpools where the river rushes into the gorge a mile from the sea, terrified divers sent into the dark to retrieve them at slack tide. Stories come to me now, not the whole truth, but true enough: Doctor D— , who came in as a patient and was put on the staff. Or the chains – the crumbling shackles my father removed from the cellars of hospital houses. I never saw the ghosts of those slaves, but my sister did: hesitant, lost – dim lights floating into place.

* * *

I remember now what our play was about: "Down in the Valley." A musical about fate, murder, and a lover who waits to be hanged. The hospital had a theatre, a whimsy of the architect, who studied Pinel. And a chapel with reversible pews, Catholic facing one way and Protestant facing the other. No one knew where the stage lights were till I found a huge double-throw switch inside a steel cage in the back: Dr. Frankenstein meet Gilbert and Sullivan. I miss that feeling of waiting for cues in the semi-dark, knowing a prairie will rise and then vanish as whole towns roll efficiently into place and the lights come up on a changed world.

* * *

I see now how Pinel's life changed the day a demented friend ran into the forest and was devoured by wolves. In years to come, how many times the good doctor must have looked out over pastoral lawns with all that before him – what madness can be. Those wolves.

They fired my father. "A cold face from the West," they called him. But not before the cook was sacked and eight hundred patients set free. Everything changed for us then. I have forgotten things he did that I swore I would never do, though I remember the cost. That and his pride. For all those souls, the ghosts put to rest, there's a lot a person ought to forgive, but it's hard. Pinel, the gentlest of men, could be reckless and utterly grim when he came to a forest.

Other Worlds

1.

How quickly one gets used to other worlds. Hidden cities, low
white buildings where light travels the corridors like a voice under
water. It's a wonder the clock still ticks. All over America there are
islands at the end of the road with their own flags. Something has
stopped: extraordinary children play and grow old in awe of the
steam plant sunk in the hill like a buried erratic. *Moron* and *Imbecile*.
These are the shades of citizenship.

2.

Staff call them hospital rats – Directors' sons, the Head Nurse's
kids. They live out of focus at the edge of the grounds, circle the
mass of the institution like small, inhabited moons. Town friends
are scared of the place. The kids make up names for the nomads
they meet on the paths – Jerry the Giant, Doug the Twirler –
second cousins from another country where *Gray's Anatomy*
doesn't exist. There are so many signs that speech can't push
through.

3.

This island rises at dawn: a village of mutes and over the bridge
there's a village of children. There's a hole in the fence near the trees
where the malformations recede like root words in the ancestral
tongue. *Mongol* or *barbaros*: other. A people can live for a thousand
years with no past tense. This tribe has no word for normal.

Coal Harbour Psychiatric

I.

I would never go to myself for counselling: so I
warn my students on their two-week rotation. All I
know is one long story, the one I'm telling now.
Norman Bethune, in his days before the Long
March with Mao, wrote of all the mistakes he made
in surgery. Who would dare these days to be so
radically wrong, if only to uphold the oath, "Do no
harm."

2.

The town contracts as each ward closes. Patients
move out: homecoming forty years after, their
parents dead and everything changed. They rush to
their freedom, precocious as children. Others stare
long and hard at faces they feel they should know.
They are wary in stores, grip their purses in both
hands. They live with strangers and pay for their
keep. Who knows where they'll be when they die?
How long before there are friends?

3.

This place has stories: the day I taught Leo to speak, or the girl I found sitting in a darkened White Cross kitchen, who calmly said, "I am thinking of jumping off the bridge," and meant it. I wasn't supposed to be there but I was. I took her out for Chinese food. She pretended we were out on a date and I played along. She laughed as we drove around in one a.m. fog that made me miss exits as I searched for her place. I made a few calls in the morning "just in case" and they increased her meds.

We are often paralyzed by doubt, while ignorance leads us to action. So far I've told you the truth and it isn't heroic. But that night feels true.

4.

I once knew a man who spent the day weeping. *Outpatients* called it a relapse. He made two cups of tea, said he was glad to see me as he apologized for his empty fridge. It glowed inside – sea-foam green, like a landscape by Magritte with an orange and a can of milk. His hands shook and he showed me a violin he was trying to make from Popsicle sticks. Didn't know when he last ate. We got him a pension. In a month he was going for beer at the Legion. The story became a legend of sorts but things are almost never so easy. Illness becomes its own scar. The only cure is trust in the long haul.

5.

The darker the ward, the darker the humour.

I love the way the patients clown and say with a
snort so the whole world can hear, "Doctor I'm
crazy, not stupid." I suppose their voices laugh too.

6.

Our stone church was built by a mason who signed
himself in. God told him to do it, an act of faith or
a penance perhaps. He never said which. Ask any
patient: demons are real, so why not an angel?

7.

Every generation, we get an artist, a real one. Years
later, demolition work on the wing is stopped in its
tracks by a dozen leaching murals. Conservators
come with scaffolds, boxes of Q-tips and alcohol, a
one-week media wonder. Spit, they say, is the best
cleaner. Cameramen wander the tunnels, shining
their lights on the ceiling like kids in a pirate cave.

Art knows the enemy here. My friend, the poet: his life is a map of all the apartments he lived in, hopes and near misses. All the burned bridges. Some days I'm one of them. "The bloody Philistines come over the hill, pound on their shields, and everyone runs for the border," he says, so knocked out with the cocktail of meds he can hardly hold a pen. "That's not for me." He shakes his shaggy head at all the disasters, another poet's passing, the world gone to hell. "It's like rivets popping on the deck of the Titanic."

8.

Slim, with black hair, Stella at nineteen had a voice like an angel, but the clouds came down. She tried slitting her wrists but just messed them up and hasn't sung since. Forty now, "Stella has a fella." Name's Jim. She has a job, he doesn't, and she tells Doctor D—, "None of your business." Way to go, Stella.

Like a blue star, love bestows a certain kind of luck. Perhaps they will get it right. (See Chapter 3 of *Love's Little Book of Mistakes*. Close to the end: "What if Love Lasts" and "The Cynics Were Wrong." But cynics won't read it.)

When they're on the outs, people conspire to bring Jim and Stella together – invitations to supper, jobs requiring the two of them: moving things into a house lit only by candles. Sometimes chance needs a hand. As for romance, it's not as rare as we think.

9.

This place is closing. They say it belongs to another
time. It could be a jail, a museum: there are such
places, but who would come to see a root cellar the
size of a school room, what it's like to be buried
under a hill? The morgue has its charms, say, or
those rotting tubs from the days of cold water
baths. Yes, even Hell has a history.

If nature's the healer, where's nature here?

10.

I say flatten it – leave a plaque in the ground, a gate
for the thousands of souls pouring through.
Sometimes I see them, a silhouette army frozen in
slashes of light on the avenues. I feel how it watches,
cloistered and gothic: two hundred windows when
the lights go out and shadows rush to the place
where light once spilled: the penumbral moon on
the old road to town as the warm dust waits for
their footsteps: the lover, the mason, the girl who
walks safely over the bridge.

JAKE

Jake comes from a lost race
of giants – forest dwellers
who walked out of the forest:
so the boy believes.

"Dig a hole here," Staff says.
Jake digs and keeps on digging. Staff
tells him to stop. "How are you going to
get out of that hole, Jake?"
Jake looks up grinning, the form
of an uneasy thought in his mind as he shifts
from foot to foot, his black
running shoes soaked by groundwater as it
gushes into each huge print.

The boy – what does he make of it?
That in a day, Jake can make a hole deeper
than a man. "Planning to sleep
in there, Jake?" Staff says.
"Staying for lunch?"
If reason is all that counts, the boy
is older than Jake, feels a child's
instinct to protect.

A muscle
does what is asked.
Jake is already part
of a child's history of remembering.
Years from now the boy
will dig his own garden, look
where the blade of the shovel
frowns as it stands in the dirt. He already senses
the way lives graze one another – we look back
through dark matter, try to find
where we are. Anomalies
in the wave fields of Heaven.

"The more there is of liberty," says M. Pariset, physician to the largest lunatic hospital in the world, "the more numerous are the chances of mental derangement..."

— *Insanity and Insane Hospitals (medical journal)*, 1837

It is better for all the world if instead of waiting to execute degenerate offspring for a crime or to let them starve for their imbecility, society can prevent those who are manifestly unfit from continuing their kind.... Three generations of imbeciles are enough.

— *Judgement on the Sterilization of Carrie Buck, Justice Oliver Wendell Holmes, Jr.*

VISITING DAY

after a photograph by Diane Arbus

I am the mouth with no sense of a face.
The boy with the solid eyes.

I'm the head a malevolent God
put on the wrong body

(if you didn't fear Him before
better start now).

You don't work here do you? Let's
go for a walk.

Sure it stinks, the blistering stench of piss, the scum
on the wall, but it's your wall after all – you built it.

This is better – the children's room, just
a bench, couple of gables, and the roof slopes to the floor.

No one's in it, which is why I come.

For your own good you should know
there's nothing that can't be stolen.

Gotta smoke?

I should warn you about Doctor Elias,
the ECT fairy.

Forget those mood elevators to the second floor.
Don't cry too much unless you're in Group (which is progress).

And don't drink the paint,
they've got files for a reason.

Personally, I like the morgue – nice place to be
if you're down.

Relax, it's a joke.
Gotta smoke? Got one for later?

Fed up, so you say?
Disenchanted with beauty?

No one worries
about "beautiful" here:

"Paint the fucking flowers
or we'll plug in your brain and turn on the juice."

Oh yeah, I can tell you lots about Art.

Ignorance isn't a problem with me, I was
born in the dark.

Want the rest of that smoke?

Hospital Dog

this yellow dog
lives like a cartoon
has just as many lives

that turn on the crackling of leaves
or the way elms wait for winter

just so the world
understands, this dog
would never fetch sticks, likes
his bread buttered

he scuttles and slides
wheeling back to the whistle
of the kid with the crewcut
who has made it this far by himself

nothing is easy and nothing is clear
in the real world of dogs
there is only today

and every dog knows how to use it

In the Heyday of Mental Health

we will make films and travel the country. Those
who lie in their beds like Lazarus
will rise from the Land of Catatonia, walk
down the hall and arrive at the cafeteria in time
for lunch. B.F. Skinner will replace voodoo
with science. Psychiatrists will take their own
medicine. LSD will be blest.

A tribe of entranced professionals
will burn their hospital whites
and go forth in street clothes like the normal,
classless civilians we all want to be. They will declare
Patients' Rights. The day pass, the group home, the
sheltered workshop, and community psychiatry
will all be invented. The lights
will come on. The menu will change,
goddammit. And social workers
will be hired.

In the heyday of Mental Health, there will be
so much optimism that patients will think
their doctors are nuts.
There will be fears, fear
that you can't unlock all those
doors, sign people up
for the crapshoot of life.

The machinery of the Dark Age
will lurch to a halt with smoke coiling from its ears.
The sand in the gears will be its own
grinding irrelevance.

So hire another fundraiser.
Build four miles of snow fence. Saviours!
Apostles from Skinner to Szaz,
meet the epiphany of Acid.
"The road is for all."

MOTHER

Where does it start? Gently,
in May. A blossoming plum outside the church as
the window beside us vibrates, an opal: Jordan River
rendered in glass and you call me a liar because
I say I can't see the blue water flowing. *Really* flowing.
You cover your ears when you think you're alone:
> *shut up*
> *shut up*

And then your famous black valentine
I Love U Mom, green stems pasted into
letters L and M, and white poppy blossoms
weeping blood.

It starts with the teachers, the social
workers – they sympathize, they talk,
you burst into tears for no reason, and they talk.
It starts with moving from school to school, with pills,
with birthday parties for one, with wild rides to
hospitals, and private schools that last for a while
because they have to.

Once I believed: *A life of my own,*
not this numbness. I want
to take pleasure again in our garden,
to believe that a sentence
won't shatter like glass, just once
I want to say *I would like...*
I would like to drive myself to the lake,
to roll by fields massing with coneflowers,
to read late on the porch as moths bunt the light,
the fluttering page caught by a zephyr.
I would like to spend a week breathing music,
to play tunes I've been missing for years.
All I ask is one day to think, to lie
in the afternoon sun, nothing but light in my eyes,
and hear the laughter I grieve for.

RECEIVING

She was receiving the night they thought the shock treatment killed
her and they went into the hall to decide whether to call the
morgue and she staggered out of the room / didn't know her own
name a permanent case of the shakes

She was receiving the time she got beat up and her sister took her
to Emergency and the cops came took a look / figured she was too
crazy to put on a stand so they shook the guy down then let him go

Then they cut her job not really a job just a program or something
she was on welfare so they cut the program or something / she
never figured out what

Sometimes she wasn't receiving at all / it was simply part of the
drift like the time her brother caught her in the barn and threw her
out the loft because she said she would tell and she did tell so he
threw her like he promised / a long way down to a couple of bales
as if he cared

She was receiving the day that minister came to her door / *Do you
believe in Jesus* and she said *I do* and he said *Do you believe in Satan*
and she said *Yes* and he said he could see Satan Satan all around
sowing and reaping / then the preacher was gone her savings were
gone but he sure left her Satan / but Satan doesn't need savings so
he hung around

She took up whispering to angels angels whispering to her / her
niece was possessed her husband possessed so she lunged after him
with the deer knife / said he sent demons to scourge her

She was receiving loud and clear behind her bolted door where she paced for weeks shouting at visions / she spread salt on the counter to keep them away but the visions seethed and the taps dripped venom and she got holier and holier

After a time everyone got old / her father got old her kids grew away the best years gone and not much ahead / Jesus was patient Satan got mellow and bridges stopped burning

Let's just suppose / suppose you are her and some relative drives you to hospital / they wire you into their system turn up the juice leave you for dead / suppose you get beat up bad and the cops arrive putting their notebooks away / suppose you give someone everything and they vanish and leave you a handful of boiling mist

And suppose the person you marry leaves you and people come and they leave you / and your children leave you and everyone leaves you / suppose your life burns out the way a house gets burned out / freezers full of rotten meat / collapsed drawers your soaked winter coat smashed plants / your children's birth certificates / Mickey Mouse clock on top of a poisonous heap / the melted face ticking one...one...one

If you weren't receiving you'd think this is Hell where everyone's staring the way people stare at a real bad accident / if you weren't receiving this would hit you hit you harder than anything / ashes / no ashes / nothing could convince you this isn't Hell and it goes on forever / not being dead receiving's the only thing bearable / receiving all the time even in sleep / in you and through you as you waltz through the daily abyss

Frowning girl, the world's a puzzled place. You might fall off this sloping lawn some afternoon. What would you leave? Wicker baskets full of washed blue shirts on days your mother took in laundry and longed for something better, her guilty kiss, the suitcase with the broken lock the day the green car came.

You were born who you are, then came through it. I haven't passed that test. Even here, you have lived; the only thing you're free from is the mask (can that be true?). My camera is my compass. If I do this right I disappear – which leaves you here, alone, among these shadows on the face of reason.

FROWNING GIRL

after an untitled photograph by Diane Arbus, a State home in Vineland, New Jersey, c. 1970

They stop for a dance although they are late. I guess it's the rouge, the tinsel wands that must have worked fine in Fairyland. I don't know why I see them this way, like broken-hearted spirits dressed in ways they would never dress themselves – a tired innocence.

This girl with her head tossed back, arm bent, looking up, looking down: surely she knows it – the way a body wants to move. Like that first crackling film: Isadora out on the arbor, nervous it seems about the way the medium jitters. Her dancers in white come forth from the wings and doors open that will never close again.

FOUR WOMEN, HALLOWEEN

*after an untitled photograph by Diane Arbus,
a State home in Vineland, New Jersey, c. 1970*

My Dear Picasso

You never dreamed
I'd come this far.

I hear you laugh as I don this diamond suit
and think of you. Those years have gone,
now there's only me, an audience of one.
But one is enough to cast a shadow on the grass,
to look into the eye of the world which is always so full
of unhappy questions.

When I was young they say it took ages, but one day
I stood up and walked,
a balance inside me.
I want you to know I have friends. They ask so little;
I want so much I'm almost ashamed.
I have no answers to painterly questions.
I move through the day. I touch, I remember.

after an untitled photograph by Diane Arbus
Vineland NJ state home, c. 1970, a costume party

Hospital Camp

Emily sits alone on a dune each night after supper, sings the few sounds she knows to this ancient, diluvian waterline sprinkled with pines.

The air over the bay darkens and waits for the moon, the last pair of pinwheeling wings. The sky cools in phrases; there is nothing to speak of. The din of the camp settles down: "rest time," when everyone listens. Staff children stand like deer in a space in the treeline; at the end of the dock, two girls lie on their bellies, reach through the reflections of their own faces and make their fingers walk along the bottom. Years from now they'll return to this shore, pick up a handful of sand. Not to hold on, but to come back to a place and once more let go of what has been lost.

Emily can't tell you the year or say, as she grins when you mention her name, if she has regrets. She has only this sense of the eloquent world. One vowel at a time.

II

The ILLUSTRATED
STATUE of LIBERTY

Statue of Liberty, Undated

My flame is just sunlight and rivets. Bronze clouds race westward like scarves freed in the wind. Who set the distance here in my eyes? I wanted to tell you, a century is both heavier and lighter than you think.

Repoussé

I dream through the night: my body in pieces as it bends around frames. Men lift a crucible, pour it gingerly into a mould. They are making the fold inside my ear which no one but the birds will see. All through the morning, dust floats to the ceiling. I feel hands constantly rubbing, a slowly growing polish of light. Far away, a half-door opens; the spokes of a cart roll out of sight as a young girl sings. My future, I decide, must be made of endless patience.

Ellis Island 1900

We come *With-Out-Papers.* WOP. They say we don't know yet: we rush from our berths – six to a room – to see the first land. We are headed for Ellis, *Island of Tears.* Papers marked with a cross or a *kikle:* Kike. A circle of chalk on a shirt. *This way, Jew. Up these stairs.* This is the way History begins.

PHOTOGRAPHER 07322

Female immigrants undergoing eye examination at Ellis Island, 1911.
KEYSTONE VIEW COMPANY, Ellis Island Series

Excerpts from the Twenty-Nine Questions

Where did you come from?
Where will you go?
What do you assume?
What star grazed the cusp of the moon when you were born? Was
the doctor a Christian? Was the volcano erupting and why did the
street built by Hadrian turn into pudding, swallowing houses and
horses and carts? Who started the war, how much did your mother
get for her rings, where did you hide your food when the soldiers
came? Who hid the dog? Any family history of idiocy?
Amputations?

What do you think of when you write your name, is there a sound
like wind rushing? A field ticking in the heat, or no sound at all?
Which eye do you favour, the left one, the left one looking into
syntax – ribbons of consonants flowing into your brain, ellipses,
spacing, longitudes of the seen, all the minutiae, every sentence you
read, or reason itself, if not, what? A light show glimmering in the
occipital crossing? Or do you prefer the right eye, the one that
follows the falcon, descendant,
                    Horus/horizon
cut by the night when the sickle moon rises:

            a desert lion hurries, her belly sags as she canters;
        out of sight, her prey races past turquoise ghosts of grass,
        crosses a knoll and goes on into continuance.

Were you there? Did you hear animal moaning in Jardin des
Plantes? Have you stood before Rousseau's *Tropical Storm with Tiger* –
seen what the beast sees? Rain-ripped foliage, a pounding white
storm. Deaths that are meant to be deaths. Were you appalled by
the mob, by the freedom? Were you so desperate? Did you leave
quickly? Tell me, what did you see?

GRAVE OF JOHN RICE

St. Raymond's Cemetery, the Bronx

Have you a name? Did we meet in the mill, working the door where the wagons come in? It seems I remember you stood at the end of a table and your voice rose over the thrum of a ship ...*heir of Dunvegan/with your pipes and your chanter/*Ho hi ri's no hi iù o/ *'Se mo rùn an t-oighre òg/*it is I who come/to a whistle from your fingertips.

Lower me down.

> *I feel him near, the very weight of me. My father's voice. Things he knew about horses. A changeable sea of a man with one thousand stories and none of his own – well he knew it. In a borrowed grave, lower him down. – Tom Rice*

How late it is. I dreamt I saw lamps in the windows guiding me home as I walked Dens Brae, the smell of jute oil thick in my clothes. I strolled down Water Street, tide turning the stones as it rushed from the river and some dark thing moved up the shore, black hooves shedding their weight as they faded into the distance, the silence that followed them sending to know why I had not come to my calling.

> *Watch me fly. I swing from the rope in the loft as you muck out the barn. When I do fly, a fork leaps out of the straw. Clean as a whistle, the tine pokes up through the top of my shoe like a canvas hook, keeps pushing through as the fork falls back. I'm frozen on the spot, mouth open. My shoe fills with heat.*

*Did you realize your habit as you held my foot in the
bowl, the way you kept moving your body between mother
and me? Blood and the soap, the water barely done boiling,
burning more than the hole in my foot. Worse than the
pain, I couldn't think why you'd do it. Needed to hear you
say this scalding wasn't your anger, it wasn't your way to
explain. – Tom Rice*

Saratoga and Constant William. I learnt the sires four lines back of
every horse I've broken. The times of a hundred more. Nervous
spirits. I see their eyes, the speed they hold back when the tip of the
whip touches their flanks and they turn, hidden and massive as
continents at the end of the longrein.

There was a time I swore I was done with other men's horses,
Margaret watching from the windows of old Higgins' house. I never
dreamt it would take so long to get out. Flesh grieves for flesh and
that's how I left her. With a mouth full of silence and young
Thomas with me.

Lower me down.

State of New York Record and Certificate of Death

> *Childbirth*
> *Convulsion*
> *Hemorrhage*
> *Gangrene*
> *Meningitis*
> *Necrosis*
> *Tetanus*

*Physician. Death has many causes.
But none of these is sufficient.*

Fell? I never fell from a thing in my life! That flash of sail, all stars and white. Water, black as an anchorstone. And Tom shouting as he brings it around. Black-hearted River. Driving her nails into my lungs. Christ. Christ in a snowstorm.

Christ take me down.

> John Rice, age 67, on Christmas Day while sailing with his son, fell into the Hudson River. Died December 26, 1903 at 10:30 a.m., John Hood Wright Memorial Hospital. Oedema of Lungs – Lobar Pneumonia.

Sometimes an animal lies – that stud that broke into a gallop when we came into the barn, tried to take off my head on the beam. I grabbed the whip and got right back on, rode him, wheeling within an inch of his life, big clots of mud and manure exploding over the fence. In half an hour that brute was penitent. He always stood quiet when I came in the stall. Though he never took his eyes off me.

> You make your home where you bury your dead. "Forget me, Tom." That's what you said. I sat all night, the pause after a breath growing longer as you slipped away. I was sure you were gone. Then you gripped my arm, as you did when I pulled you out of that freezing spray – and you called out "Nellie! What's wrong old girl?" And fell back dumb. – Tom Rice

Inside my head. Like sleeping beside a river thundering – chestnut stallions. My sweet little Bay giving her heart over and over and fighting her way through the field. It was her pride – she could never hold back.

The snow's grace is fragile, its warmth erasing the shame of the solitude, the graves with stones and those with none. The prayer rises visible up through my breath. "Críst i ngin cech òin immurorda/Críst i cech cluais rodom-chlothar/Christ in every mouth that speaks my name, every ear that hears me." For my father's life come to this earth with a bit of pressed thistle, a handful of oats still in his pocket. This morning, the 29th of December, as I ease him, ease him down. – Tom Rice

Improvisations on Mr. Foster's *New York Standard Guide*

(Width of mouth 3'0")

The heart travels blindly and mostly alone. What can we know? Truth is not history.

(Index finger: 8'0")

Love, last night I dreamed you stood at the foot of my bed, watching as I slept, your feet were bare and you walked slowly, and slowly your hands passed over me like rough cloth; the floor creaked in one room, then another; all through the house the boards were trying to remember some gesture or weight. The sash nudged the sill and the walls sighed, or I thought they did, as the moon slid over them, the tips of your fingers brushing my skin, circling beneath me as my breath escaped.

(Ground to tip of torch, 305'1")

This island sees you: passing
with only the clothes on your back.

Am I, then,
the beacon? Say a word,
and that is the word I will be. I am
what you made me: Voicefulness watching.

ON THE STAIRS

Keystone View Company
Ellis Island Series, Photographer 13502

It was the worst idea I had in my life and I get three words from Meadville: *I like it*, signed B.L. Singley, himself.

I'm all set up at the top of the steps, the first boatload comes through the gate as the breeze picks up the smell of people ten days at sea. The front of the wave hits with their cases and sacks, and I have to run in front of the camera just to keep them from knocking it flat.

Some *opa* stops halfway up the stair, his wife is trying to drag him the rest of the way, but the Immigration men don't miss a trick. "This way", they say as they haul him to quarantine and his cursing wife too – none too easy gripping her arm. The crowd pushes ahead and you can bet no one's going to stop now.

I ask what it's about and the guy on the door says, "Look Paddy, if they stop on the stair, their lungs are no good. We don't need whatever disease they've got. If they look kind of white it's TB. If the wife's loaded down, carries the heaviest bags, you're looking at a bad heart. If they limp and they tell you they're fine, that could mean TB in the leg, an ulcer or maybe gangrene. If they can't see – and believe me, lots are blind as a bat – they hesitate like they can't read the signs or they're lost, and it's back on the boat. Then you got criminal types and your A-symmetricals. You got men who look like women; you got women who look like men; some don't want to look you in the eye. Sometimes they just don't look right and you can't put your finger on it, but you know they ain't right: weasels."

"Also, if they've got a chalk circle on the collar, those are the Jews. Don't care what colour they are as long as they're Christian. If they're sick and got kids, the kids go through this door. If the parents go back, the kids go back. Lots are related, so if they've got an uncle who's jake on this side, the kids can stay. We got twelve thousand a day. The main thing is: look in their eyes. And keep right on looking."

Pictures? You better believe it, B.L.

Theory of Love
Keystone View Company, Western Vista Series

PHOTOGRAPHER 10459

a.

I have taken pains with this picture, *Love, Courtship and Marriage*. I
expect it to sell. A groom and a bride framed in a mirror – the
perspective's arranged, pulling you in past two figurines: *it is this far
across the table.* I am proud of the plausible touch, the way the eye
travels to make you believe. The corner with ferns, a painted rose,
and leaves on the wall: all of which say *we belong to this world.*

b.

Here is the heart of the story – stealing a kiss (even your granny
approves as she titters). A boy with his knee on a stool as he
whispers. From here on it's a labyrinth, lovers reflected in mirrors.
You choose the end. Already, you're cocking your head to see
around corners, pictures of doorways that are not really there. This
is the oldest of tricks. There are no accidents.

Montana Bison

KEYSTONE VIEW COMPANY, Western Vista Series

a.

That Sioux was right, take a picture of something and you destroy it – in your mind, I mean. Most of these buffalo, a small herd of thirty or so, are probably dead by now, and so are their kin. Now, or in a hundred years, what's here is what I want you to see: a space in the spine of this country.

b.

When these brutes move, it's no good waving your arms: *Would you please stop moving?* I worked for this picture, now I'm a legend. Which leaves you and the hoi polloi, amazed, with your face in the viewer (Saint Louis-Chicago-New York), looking backward at shadows that are already gone.

O'Neil's Point

KEYSTONE VIEW COMPANY, Western Vista Series

a.

Look at this one, a good paying job: O'Neill's Point, Colorado Grand Canyon, nineteen-ought-one. But not many dames. That idiot hanging onto a sapling and leaning over the cliff is Herb, my two-bit assistant. That girl is really his sister. I needed them there for the scale. If there's anything a camera can't stand, it's emptiness.

b.

Take something a human can understand out of a picture and even the Grand Canyon looks flat. For the kind of Big that nature supplies, you want vertigo, the idea of somebody falling. Death if possible. You want the person doing the seeing to be fifteen feet out from the cliff, looking down, then looking over at Herb and thinking: Herb, you're a goddamned idiot. That's what this job's about.

Sitting Bull and Buffalo Bill, by William Notman.

William Notman of Montreal

I have photographed Jefferson Davis in exile,

      prime ministers (most of them sober),

      Buffalo Bill,

a bosomed parade of hoteliers' wives.

Next to their jailers,

that band of ill-fated Confederate spies outside the jail.

Also this riff-raff I hire by the hour, dressed up

in deerskins so they can hunt fake moose

      with unloaded guns

and warm themselves around a painted fire

in the middle of a starlit afternoon.

            It's an art, alright.

Sitting Bull

WILLIAM NOTMAN *of* MONTREAL

PHOTOGRAPHER 10459

a.

Forget the claptrap they taught you. Begin with the surface – you owe it attention. What I believe is: questions are frivolous. Learn from the present, which allows itself to be washed away. Yet, when it leaves, leaves us the image.

b.

I will take this plate to the developing room. Perhaps I will fail. I think not – History believes in the fuse. How many Presidents resolve, "An eye for an eye"? How many answer, "Not this eye"?

Three Dancers from Senegal

start
with any language you like or
    indigo swirling
        white sand and a fish

what moves in the breath of this young girl sleeping?

how long does she stay by the water?
        how long by the river?

God's invisible Name walks like a cat
        like the moon in the desert

        tabla wolof –

        this beauty, Death
this beauty, Life

    the difference between them thin
    as a petal

        adrift
in the well of her dreaming

Dancer from Senegal (Reprise)

She needs the drumming inside, the song
submerging the madness which waits
at every turn.

She seeks worthy things, a voice
to carry her across the lake of loss,
the eyes of a stove at midnight, or the small wave of heat
that sits in the mouth of a pot.

Her home is loneliness, exile in a soundless land.
She longs for the hollow beating of life in the open air, the shuffle
of feet and the klaxon of a wheezing automobile as children pile in.

Calling for water, her thirst is not slaked.
What she craves most is that which answers her bones,
a taste of the fire as it consumes us.

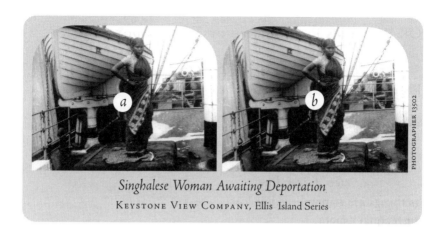

Singhalese Woman Awaiting Deportation
KEYSTONE VIEW COMPANY, Ellis Island Series

PHOTOGRAPHER 13502

a.

She puts on her future,
dusty as cinnamon. Knowing fate,
what is there to ask? For a moment
I think she will speak. I steady
the tripod, removing the cap.
You can never be tentative.
For those of you viewing

b.

she will always be waiting
on the deck of a boat
getting ready to leave.
Because of this art,
the stanchions
gleam, and the lifeboat
hangs dead on the pulley.

ON WESTON'S PHOTOGRAPH OF TINA MODOTTI, 1923

He photographs M, her skin
        is her shadow.
Her life is a single tree.

This is her doorway,
        one step descending
as things are remembered or lost
with equal weight.

Who would not wish to be
        the one for whom she poses in black,
light leafing the wall.
Everything recognized by love
is here.

Generations pass, of whom
        the world knows nothing. Then one afternoon
a sheet of light descends to the floor of the heart
                and we see how we came to its stations –
by the grace of a sleeve, or because love either stays
or it leaves, a ringless hand – and for seventy years, God waits.

Ovid

I shall continue to dwell at the edge
        of a world, a land far removed from my own.
Here it is that I am a barbarian,
        understood by nobody.

III

LEARN *to* PAINT

We must be gentle of our dreamers.

– Robert Frost

Their Daughter

The father, the mother. Between them, their daughter. He plays contract bridge, remembers each card played in a game six months back. His drink is scotch, which could mean he drinks too much, but it doesn't. It just means that his drink is scotch.

The grand house fills with the long inhalations of sliding doors. A pin turns end over end as it drops. Shhh.

> And the mother: what shall be imagined
> for her? Regrets? The failure of duty?
> The sound of constant crashing where love should be?
>
> There should be a saying,
> and there is: Save yourself.
> She's heard it before.

Their daughter is here, Faith, who drew before she could talk.

At sixteen, she stretches canvas on a six-foot frame, the floor splashed with gesso. For reasons now lost, she paints the Statue of Liberty, the harbour sky streaked with plumes of apocalypse. Down Liberty's blue-grey face, the track of a palette knife. The folds of her gown crack as she sinks in a pile of skulls. Liberty Island-Golgotha: the world cast in cement. Nothing could fly in those skies. Even madness held back.

And now, as if freed from an errant dream, the mother chooses the day she will leave this tableau in search of the rest of her life. Beyond the horizon, the Mother of Exiles moves in the mind as a mountain might move, by ascension.

Learn to Paint

Faith

1.

This room looks like hell.
You know how I live – one day to the next.
I find a surface, it wears me down.

What choice is there? I work
on the painting, the big one.
I consider the attack – clear in my mind.
Each stroke comes down
like the armourer's hammer.

2.

Start with a gesture, let your hand, without looking
follow a shoulder, a back. Learn
to work quickly: forget just as fast.
Space has a colour.
A line always moves
away from its weight. Let it leave.
Take a step back and see what you are:
just a motion. Nothing else is
and nothing else matters.

3.

Next you must list
all that you owe:

The light as it came on you, the foot
you failed to caress or the mask
you say you revealed – with what? Art?
A paucity

brought you to this.
Mostly the question: What if I fail?
What if failure
is all I can do?

4.

When you are ready with
scraps of cloth and
your oil,
you must forget everything.
A moment ago you weren't ready,
but now you are.
Before the first stroke
makes the canvas bloom like the roof of a circus tent,
a bud of green paint
slides down the side of the cup into a pool,
equally green. This is the moment,
its surface is bottomless.
All you can do is begin.

5.

I was wrong.
Light will not wait.
This hour, this exhaustion
is the space you have made for attention.
It must be pulled, dragged ahead
by what you do not know.

Sacrifice choice,
give up on wisdom.
The world doesn't need another prophet.

6.

You think it's too hard. It is.

7.

Now you are ready.

Self-Portrait as the Harlot by the Side of the Road

Isn't this what
    you wanted?
        Didn't you want
to be hungry? Didn't you
    want this mouth? This veil?

        What will you leave –
    you only possess.
        The land you own you have not laboured in.
    But this blue veil you
        cannot forget.
Now I am the taste of everything you eat.

Liberty head in a park.

Liberty (study)

Life, if it lives here,
      borrows the form,
something to speak through. I don't know
the words, but this is the way I talk
when I paint, seeking exhaustion. I want to see clearly,
to have nothing left, not even emptiness.

This line is the shore where a statue will grow,
I choose a woman but this
      is simply appearance.
She's a skeptic in the ancient sense
that life cannot be known, and sometimes justice
isn't poetic. She believes we make our own knowledge,
that freedom is as common as bread,
which is made every day, the anthem of the ordinary.

Athena's gold was held on by rivets.
      But Athens was sacked and
the statue is gone.
My *Keeper* is covered in copper,
      her iron armature is a delicate business with many flaws.
She believes truth must be rescued from philosophy;
      the gods can't be blamed for our weakness.

I once saw a statue – it was not in this country – *The Seven Heroes of October*. It stood in a sunny courtyard but it was impossible to go near because of the bees. No one knows how, but over the years the bees learned to build their hive in the statue, too high for the gardener to reach. This is God's little joke, and a good one: "These seven are dead and you are alive; everyday, like these bees, you must watch over Liberty."

As if they were children, their happiness inevitable as morning's first zephyr, they entered the harbour, a place for a temple. They began with a tree and a vine: histories begin where water quietly laps the shore.

After the wars came marble and slaves, olives and wine. They moved out in every language. "We are the map," they said, "We are the sea."

But their enemy lived in the market, he worked in their fields. He came in colours they knew too well. It was their turn to pay. They staggered on foot through the passes, left their dead for the dogs they could not kill.

They smelled the roofs of Athens burning and swore "We'll return." They found a root growing up through the shards of the temple: History's skeptical fugitives saved by a shoot from the corpse of a tree. Then it all changes: the temple, the gods, the tree.

IN THE DARK

At Easter, Faith paints the three women

In the grey before morning

when dust weighs the residue

I must paint...

The women bring aloes,

myrrh for the body

Mary of Magdala, you will be here

as a door creaks and a bolt rattles into place beyond the frame

Your eye remembers, comes closest to me

fear is familiar in the landscape of madness

Wife of Clopus, I've hidden your face

The bundle tucked in a fold

where everything vanishes –

you hide this weight like a thief

Who turns to you, Joanna

        what hastens you on

    All I have is one truth

       you never were lovely

  no lovely bones

        Your name, like a breath

     will soon be forgotten

The guard by the tomb awaits you

need awaits you

This darkness could go on forever

Tony

How do you make love to a mad woman? In top hat and cape, ride through her country on a penny farthing, coasting down hills, an eccentric path winding through fields of inky flowers. The petals are white she says, because she can't take the colours.

She comes to your room, her tanned feet cross the floor to the window where the breeze blows in from the bay. You catch the loop of her belt in your fingers, pulling her down as she laughs *how clumsy you've become*. She is stronger than you, but thin, like a bird catching its breath before it is gone, *do not forget me* whenever she holds you. The scent of the future clings to her skin. She is making you lucid.

Meeting

The magic hour creeps through the graveyard.
        The light and the dark, the years
have worn the crumbling stones
        just as the dead wear out sleep.

The dead sense all the possibilities, how things uncoil,
        go around, elegant and predictable.
If they dream at all, they dream simply of a scored stone bench
        where strangers depart as strangers.

A man and a woman meet – no names.
        She gazes at the hospital across the street,
"The Misery" she calls it, lights a cigarette, says
        she'd give anything not to be here.

There is more strength than beauty in those storms in her eyes,
        her laugh is an elegy to laughter long past.
He leans toward her, smiles – that's all; she loves
        the grace which is his, it gives him away.

There's a glimmer, the kind ephemeral light
        that's seen a long way off through trees.
It warms them although they don't know it;
        there is so much ahead it must bring them through.

LIKE BRANCUSI

Faith

I see you walk
your presence weighs everything
hard objects yield, and the floor
has a secret spring.

You move with this world.
A river that passes, and still
the river remains.

Your body's a tower
where every cell's locked until it is touched.
Hard to know. Difficult,
curving. It trembles as my breath
passes over it.

Like Brancusi's *Bird in Space,*
it is the kind of form
a room is made for.

Railroad Dreams

Tony

I.

If not for the light on the tracks, our trust in the vessel
        which bears us from one dispossession to another,
if not for forgetting
                we could not bear ourselves.

The night is full of last stops. The blackening wind breathes
through stacks of crushed cars the way an old man draws air
through his teeth. This is the country kept from us, the blur of
fugitive trees,
                        yards and abutments
                where balconies rust above diesel-soaked ground.

We enter the world, it strips us down.

2.

We move undercover, disguising the cracks in our presence,
suspicious of strangers, while the stranger inside us wants to engage
all comers: the face in the mirror when the momentum swings like
a weight on a string or the line through the heart of a story – any
story:

A man marries a woman with a nervous disease. Her martyred
mother confides to anyone who will listen that her daughter is
mad. *And with her condition, well... children are out of the question.*
The mother nurses a smoldering indignation, which she covers
with a layer of ash and icy manners. A seed has been planted
and after a year the man wonders if he has made a mistake.
They argue about children, about money, rehearse in their
minds the long list of failures. Some days are good, they think
they'll pull through, then there's a miscarriage – the end of the
last solid ground. They try to speak and conversations break off
like branches weighed down by ice. Under their breath, they
whisper *leave, why not leave.* The woman's condition gets worse,
there is no ending. This kind of outcome is common.

3.

The train rattles on through the unfocused scenery. It believes in a world which cannot be seen from the tracks. The hundred-ton body wants to leap from its bed, to veer from its own gravity, one mass leaving another, an anomaly in the heavens – a radio star revolving like a beacon in the blue dome of the station, a source of distortion which has to be checked against the ticket, the luggage tags, and the blinking light of the place which is known.

4.

Love on a train is a current which flows from one end of the car to another, the embrace which lingers longer than it has to in the suffocating passage between cars as our bodies lurch randomly together and the strobing light passes through us, harmless as a magician's sword. If only there were somewhere to hide, if night would come or the sun not take so long to set. A caress? If only we could mould ourselves like chrome, our bodies polished as windows, lightly whipped by the shadows of branches. We return to our seat. Your legs press against mine as you slice the skin from a peach, its body revealed, sunny and streaming, as you lick the edge of the open knife. You press the pit in my hand, laugh as you hold it there.

5.

We dream of arrivals, exhaust and the smell of a tunnel. We race for a roof-high heap of identical cases. Green light spills from the baggage car. A man waves us on as we give him our tags. The bags are en route to the continent: to Brunswick, Maine; Brunswick, Maryland. Or else Montreal. We call out in French, our questions drowned by the roar of an incoming train as we pull at the pile, grasping for handfuls of improvised air.

We race through the station. Clumps of tourists with nametags laugh and shake hands, blocking the way as we vault up the escalator. A case scrapes my leg as we veer round a corner: stairs to another tunnel where another train hisses and the conductor waves and we jump for a door that is moving away. You pull me in, the conductor catches us both and the car fills with applause. We bow with a smile, rock and weave down the aisle. Leather seats sigh, we sink in.

You tell me a dream: *it's dark as you race through a tunnel. A train you have never been able to reach is pulling away.* It happens again and again. You laugh as you say you don't think you'll have that dream anymore. Our faces laugh back in the window. *Fenêtre, la vitre:* we sleep on a five-hour ride, lulled by the rocking, the hiss – cases wedged in a gleaming cage at the back of the car. The train tilts into a curve as birds rise from the neck of a lake, itself like a swan, a black one. There's a space, a far-off sigh. *Billet Madame! Billets!* One at a time, our bags disappear with a small puff of steam.

WEIRD CURE

Faith

Last night I couldn't sleep. All-night nerves. Then I did dream: I was in an operating room. The surgeon was probing for cancer – I thought it was cancer. My belly was open and I was awake. He worked with a clamp. We chatted, it was all of great interest, and I talked too. He tapped the needle then he gave me the shot. I trusted his skill and nothing else mattered. Not the pooling of blue on the scalpels laid on the tray, nor the halo of black outside the light. "Now she is ready," he said, as a row of chairs creaked in the balcony. Then I slept, slept like the dead.

Tony Again

Because I stutter
      my voice is a ploughed field,

I cross it walking backward
      in the dark. Even this can be learned.

If this is a stage
      the trapdoor is open.

Some say, to stumble with words
      means something: not always.

When I work, each word's rehearsed
      until there is light around it.

How I got here is a long story, I'll just say
      I wear my flaw on the outside.

This is what I do.
      I write.

DEAR MISS INVISIBLE,

I love your logic
which is transitive of nothing,
        like the shape of a leaf on
a tongue, almost nothing.

Elusive shade, I wear you
all day like a shadow
                inside my body
which is nothing.

What comes after and only before: a jewel on velvet,
a pearl in the sea? You say this knowing
        what I love most is a mystery, something to solve
in the afternoon's mulatto light.

So let the blind down, let down the night
to better enjoy your element, which is
                weightless but claims me
like an unlit planet: anticipation.

NUDE

Niagara Falls region

So near the rapids.
So near the wonders of the world.

At the time I was tired,
I worked and everything fit.
In this civilized shade you found me
with what the afternoon contains.
Nothing but subject.

When a woman paints a woman
she considers herself.
It has nothing to do
with description. Not
these bare
forking branches, nor ferns –
tongues of the obvious world
reduced to a ground.
Take the varnish, take the grandeur,
take the blue spirit mountains.
We are mostly a shadow
under the skin.

I could change this landscape
at a whim: I own everything.

Experiment with an Air Pump

My love, you're the child with the air pump, a precocious student of nature who elegantly proves that, starved of oxygen, a white parakeet kept under a bell jar will die.

Given time, you will unravel the mysteries of the heart, how many times a minute it beats, how it behaves the instant before it bursts, before it finally sighs like an antique locomotive and simply keels over. As you say, it's not a question of kindness.

I write this from the Hotel Castillano. The band from Quito is playing and the trumpeter in the chalky suit gazes this way. His Cimmerian eyes settle on me the way a pair of birds settle on a telephone wire when they're about to move in. His frail voice concedes I am already part of the repertoire. His eyes watch *the fire*, in Spanish the song goes *if it isn't satisfied now, it will surely die later*. How can one resist such insatiability, the jaded song of existence, which reduces itself to a couple of favourite bars and finally staggers home, defeated by its own body.

I wish you the very best of luck with that pump and the pointless curiosity with which you are so well equipped. But suppose that everything can be reduced, that God leaves Her crib notes lying around for you to find: would God really care about answers She already knows?

Can you hear the air rush back into the jar? I hear it plainly. I wish life could get back to where it was, if only that dumb, extinguished bird could get up and start walking. That would be science. That would be a method God could respect.

Found Poem

"Bone." I wrote "bone" in your hand. You were talking
so much that day that it sounded like a crying of bones. I was sad.
Our bodies must have been unquiet.

Father Aesop

Faith

My grandmother's bed smells like
wool and a mothball, but it's
going to sleep I'm afraid of.
I say, Daddy, tell me the story
about me and the Saracens, yes
I promise I'll sleep

> There once was a girl (yes, it was you) just a
> regular girl, except that her parents were clams, she
> had seaweed for hair and a pearl for a bellybutton.
> She was kidnapped by Saracens on their way home
> for supper. They thought that a girl with seaweed for
> hair and a pearl for a bellybutton should fetch quite a
> ransom, but lucky for her, her sea cow grew legs and
> wandered away and found her way home, but not
> before making the rank of sergeant in the foreign
> legion and crashing her Sopwith Camel into a dune....

Everything happens twice, the tale
pratfalls into an ending
which sets the girl free,
a story I cling to
when I lie in a nervous bed,
wondering when we gave up
on blue-footed birds diving into the waves,
on stealing away
in a boat with the moon on its sail.

I think I should write to those Saracens
and thank them.

Old Family Film

Nude men swimming like swales
pull themselves onto rocks, marvellous
and white. They sun themselves and shiver, their skin
sparkles like fresh-cut marble. Foam splays like a net,
rakes the beach and hisses uphill, stones crackle.
Out of sight there is laughter.

There are times when statues speak; the sun
swirls until the sky is wound hard above a harder sea.
Men shout as they run into waves in twos and threes and dash out.
They are neither young nor old and they talk – there is always
a story to be told,
a song so old it can only be hummed.
Close your eyes and you'll hear. Look away
and you'll see.

swale: dialect word for a seal, especially a harp seal.

Thalassophilia

Faith

           More than anything, I want
to wake without a past
so that in the morning I might know the terms
that God intended. I'd leave this land for good,
the century before me
like a river in the ocean.
I would either rise
or fall among the masts and lumber,
find the place between the spars where you can see
the way the world flows –
the troughs, the tattered shirts
worn like ribbons earned on deck.
I would keep a handsewn book, learn
a verse each night until it changed,
travelling in me. There is
no way to know the rights or wrongs, how such a life
would go. No choice, perhaps,
in anything
but how we die: the land, the sea.

Unfinished Portrait

Faith

        Sooner or later, we all paint
ourselves. The person I paint
              resembles me:
        raw canvas or tin.

           I spend months
on questions of paper,
              these...ingredients.

I cannot speak
        if there is no light.
And it's true
I hear singing most of the time.

        Some paintings
refuse
          to be finished. My eyes?
              They don't
          look away.
      My looks, if I have them, are the kind that fade.
My lips are too thick, not lovely at all.
          If anything's lovely,
        let me remove it.
I loathe that I am weak, ambitious too.
          I want you to see me.

STORY OF A TREE

Faith, after a painting by Piet Mondrian

A girl draws a lollipop tree:
a stick,
green orbit above it
and two red apples – nothing's

more basic. Then she adds branches
a bird with a beak
(the sun's wearing glasses).

There's a quarter-pie window
in a funny brick house, a chimney
that sprouts teal-coloured smoke like Grandmother's hair.

The tree grows some buttons
and a rough coat of bark.
Next, leaves, on which caterpillars
(who also wear glasses)
dine. When leaves
are done being green
they thoughtfully drift
into piles on the ground.

Snowflakes stick to *The Sky*
while *Dog with a Sweater*
follows *Kids to the Hill.*

Around eight o'clock, the boughs are reduced to their lines
and scratches in the crayoned night sky reveal
three shifting stars and a galaxy much like our own.

After some travel, the tree becomes worldly,
a swirling blue cypress,
and the peaks of the houses turn into mountains.
A rise in the road sheens in the moonlight
and a girl whose loosened mantilla
shies from the bone, baring
her neck, hurries
by argentine fields.

The fields disappear in the seasonal bending,
the landscape cools and concludes it is winter.

The mist becomes snow,
the kind that envelops like a form of suspicion.
Just enough light stumbles over a bough
to consecrate branches.

Should a traveller pass by there is nothing to see
and less to remember.

But the tree is still here. In essence.

Untitled

Faith

Give me a name that has walked,
waits for the other, knows: *this is all.*

Give me Mercy any day. Drop the weights
from my arms and my feet.

There are angels enough with messages
for busy, well-lit saints.

Tell that bastard, Life,
I know you.

How many Madonnas
reach into strollers: who knows these pietas?

Give me mercy anytime.
Why not Mercy?

IV

ACTS of MERCY

Love the man and you will love the Art.

– Aphorisms of Hippocrates

The Memory Museum

My father's afraid
of walking in crowds, the strangers
who know him. His life
is full of apologies. He no longer recalls
the museum he visited every week
for twenty years. So much
is left hanging. I say to friends
who ask how he is: I hardly know myself.
The day is soon when I'll become
one of the present-forgotten.

There is a kind of forgiveness
in museums. You are asked to remember
no one. It is only
a station of time
with lives that don't
know you, you have wronged
no one, you have loved
no one, they owe you
nothing, the weight of their presence is light
and every memory is the right one.

Soon, he'll remember
less of me; we're already resigned
to what can't be recovered. We speak
like strangers bent over the same hand-tooled pot,
with regret for the missing piece that would make it perfect.

Walking the edge of the past
                    if...
          when...
the day is soon
when he'll ask my name. Do I know him?
Have I come to check the meter?
Already, he has begun to look at me
long and hard. I cannot speak,
so little is left
and someone has thoughtfully written
          Tuesday, May 9
          White pill at 1:00

A note for the two of us
becoming less.

THE SEVEN ACTS OF MERCY

the life so short,
the Art so long to learn...
the chance soon gone, experience
deceptive
–Hippocrates

1. *Caring for the Sick*

    I face each day with resolve, envy the grace of so many who cannot save themselves. I am no good at this, but better than most. My credo should be: The mistakes I have made, I will make again.

    How long can one live – paralyzed from the heart down? I lately feel I've crossed over, walk like a soul among resonant selves, the dead and the living. I will learn everything this time around. Words come back and how slight they seem: *Do no harm, care for the body.* But I feel their weight as I feel the ground. Christ knows who's the patient here.

2. *Visiting Prisoners*

Everything is a calculation: where to sit so the manic won't rush up with her questions. The assault of her conversation makes claims on your shattered life. Meantime, your sister asks, "Would you like toast? Coffee?" These are the privileges your visit brings. How safe it all seems. The gleaming floors, plaques screwed onto the furniture – vinyl and chrome. The walls are colour-coded: *this way off the ward.* A four-hour pass, a ten-hour pass: how much is it worth to be this side of freedom? Even now, the nurses are watching. Are you coming or going?

3. Refuge to Pilgrims

> Everything counts on the margins of love, the way
> we shudder when touched or stop in the middle
> of dressing, alarmed by a voice in the hall. We're forbidden
> the places we love in, the gardener's shed or the alcove under
> the stair going down to the steam plant. It's a war –
> the way we live marking time by the rumble we feel through the wall.
> The night shift changes.
> Love carries on while no one is looking.
> We ask for nothing and notice everything, think only of
> how and when, and we ask no permission, sure that
> our bodies will give us away
> as we sneak to our rooms, glowing inside.
> There's a pill for everything we do
> but we'll risk it. We are the last of the last hope of Romance,
> with nothing to lose but some sleep.
> And it's like faith, those distant detonations.
> The world's out there somewhere. Sooner or later
> someone will find it.

4. *Feeding the Hungry*

After awhile, food is a function: what attention it takes. To lift a spoon to your mouth is a victory. To chew, to swallow, is to hold on to your body. So keep the cart waiting:

> Do not go gentle
> or any other way. Weeping
> needs no explanation.
> Loved ones long dead
> die again each day. Here
> is the pudding. You could choke
> on a wafer. Body of Christ?
> If there was ever a need
> for a joke, this is it.

5 *Clothing the Naked*

He stands alone in the dimly lit room – 6:00 a.m. The other
men sleep. He is thin, like the ivory Christ in an Arctic church
(even the nails are delicate). There's a saucer-shaped dip in the side
of his head: 1953 – the lobotomy. It's why the buttons on his
pajamas seem so big, and why he lifts his clothes from the chair so
carefully. Everything must be done in the right order, in the right
way. He prefers the silence; words are like fenceposts with the wires
between them gone.

His shirt hangs away from his body – a child wearing chain
mail. And sometimes he remembers when he was a boy on a farm,
the quarter horse pulling him to school as he trailed behind on
homemade skis. His face lights up as he speaks of it, as if meeting
his own ghost. Then it's gone.

Three dollars and fifty-seven cents. He sticks his wallet in his
pants. His loafers slip on easily.

6. *Relieving the Thirsty*

No need to whisper. The doors are all closed on burn unit rooms, in every room the need for blood. Voices moaning as they drift into the wrong side of sleep, dreaming again how they bent toward the hissing furnace or ran from room to room carrying burning carpet. Electricians fallen from the sky, lie down like snow angels with holes blown in their spines.

Nurses carry trays with needles and swabs. Even they must turn away, chatter cheerily as they walk past doors, a sign this is not the much-feared knock.

I say, "Leonard?"
"Come in."

You tell me some cock-and-bull story about filling a 99-cent lighter. A lie, of course. You tried to drink it. For the first time in years you're eating three meals a day. Pain has lifted the veil of all that booze. You see me clearly, young and green, though not as green as you think. For some reason you want to give me something. Your nicotined fingers reach for the flap of a soiled envelope, shake the contents out on the pillow. You pass me a picture and tell me to keep it: *My daughter, she's all grown-up.* It makes no sense, but I take it. You'll be gone in a week. People, it seems, are always alone when they burst into flames. Tomorrow begins the long line of losses.

7. *Burying the Dead*

No one visits the graveyard next door. An iron fence, the public
stones. I think of the dead. The determined suicides walking calmly
in their last days – toward the inevitable. I think of Moira, the
signals she sent us, the little rug of a dog she bought for company,
her poems and her father's four-hour flight for the winter funeral, a
man who arrives and leaves in the dark. His voice sank as he spoke.
Our condolences shamed him: the vague eulogy for a life led mostly
in secret. But we sense the trajectory of our own, how easy it is to
make one wrong move, to close our eyes and let go of everything.
And Moira, who thinks of her now? What happens to ashes?

A Wall In Heaven

If Heaven had a wall it would be eight feet high, with a top you can reach from a stool, the one your mother used when she dusted up high. You could hang any picture you want, there would be so much variety: candlewood frames, oils from the hall of a bank, aquatints, petit point *home sweet home, may memory like the sundial mark naught but sunny hours* in a bamboo frame. Everything would somehow fit in. Think of something needed, and it would appear at that moment, making up for things left unsaid, all those times you just didn't think. A second chance.

In Heaven's illumination everything would appear as it is, in shades. The flaws of half-familiar lives looking out would be necessary for some reason known only to the wall. They might be needed so we could greet each other without guile, so we could listen as God must listen, to everything. All of the angels would travel by foot, stirring the silvery dust. It would be thought a grace to be human, to be close to life as we are now, and for that reason the loveliest angel would walk with a limp, and have downcast eyes.

Author's Notes

1. *My Days with Young Christian Players:* Phillipe Pinel's (1745-1846) humane treatment of mental patients changed the course of institutions for "the insane." He removed chains from the walls and did away with purging, blistering, bleeding, and replaced them with simple psychological treatments with startling results. The quote on Pinel is from the Schizophrenics Anonymous Forum. SA is a self-help and advocacy group. The poem is set in a psychiatric hospital in the 1960s. By the mid-1980s most institutional populations were reduced to a fraction of their former size and to specialized services. Many hospitals were closed or converted to other uses. Community supports did not follow, however, and many now swell the ranks of the homeless.

2. *Justice Oliver Wendell Holmes, Jr.:* Carrie Buck was the first person to be sterilized under the Virginia Sterilization Act of 1924. Recent scholarship shows that Carrie Buck had a false diagnosis. Far from being promiscuous, she had been raped by a relative of her foster parents. Contrary to the evidence presented in court, the daughter she had out of wedlock was "normal," and the lawyer representing her conspired with the prosecution. The history of eugenics and of sterilization laws in Canada closely followed developments in the United States.

3. *Repoussé.* This is the method used to hammer the sheets of copper into shapes, which are then riveted together. This largely forgotten art was used to create the sheathing for the Statue of Liberty and revived during the restoration of the statue for its Centennial.

4. *Excerpts from the Twenty-Nine Questions:* A card with twenty-nine questions was used to screen immigrants at the Ellis Island immigration processing centre.

5. *Grave of John Rice:* Based on the story of my great-great-grand-father, who fell into the Hudson River in a boating accident on Christmas Day, 1903. He died on the 26th. His son, Tom, returned to Scotland a few years later. Not all of the immigrants stayed. The first Gaelic quotation is from "The Young Heir," an old song of unknown origin collected by Margaret Bennett. The Gaelic fragments in the final stanza are from a prayer for protection called The Lorica (Breastplate) or The Deer's Cry, and is attributed to Saint Patrick, who was saved from an ambush by being transformed into the image of a deer while reciting the prayer.

6. *Self-Portrait as the Harlot by the Side of the Road.* In Genesis 38, Tamar, Jonathan's widow, disguises herself as a harlot to seduce her father-in-law, Judah. In doing so, she saves herself and her son from a life of servitude in her husband's clan. She is the direct ancestor of Solomon, David, and therefore, Jesus of Nazareth.

7. *Nude*: After a painting by Canadian painter, Prudence Heward, 1931. The original *Girl Under a Tree* is in the Art Gallery of Hamilton. Lawren Harris said it was the best nude painted in Canada up to that time.

8. *Experiment with an Air Pump.* This was a painting by Wright of Derby (1734-97) depicting the popular obsession with science. Two girls look on as their pet cockatoo lies dead under a bell jar, its life snuffed out by the natural philosopher in the name of science.

9. *Found Poem.* The quotation is from American photographer, Diane Arbus. She was reminding Alex Elliot what she wrote on his hand in a graveyard when they were teenagers.

10. *Thalassophilia.* Or "love of the sea." American eugenicist Charles Davenport claimed to have identified a number of genetically determined traits based on his research with immigrants at Ellis Island. He claimed that many other traits were inherited including thalassophilia, suspiciousness, obtrusiveness, feeblemindedness, industrial sabotage, pauperism, train wrecking, and skill at chess. Davenport was also the father of the IQ test, an early version of which he developed at Ellis.

11. *Story of a Tree.* The poem is inspired by the paintings of the pioneering abstractionist, Piet Mondrain (1872-1940). Mondrian had an obsession with painting a single tree; in series of paintings, the tree gradually disappears as he tries to represent the unrepresentable.

12. *The Seven Acts of Mercy:* Inspired by Caravaggio's 1607 painting, which was commissioned for the Pio Monte de Misercordia (hospital) in Naples, where it hangs today. In the Catholic tradition, the seven acts reduce one's time in Purgatory. It has been said that this complex work stirs the viewer to piety by the evidence of things in themselves, rather than by gestures or appeals to emotion.

ACKNOWLEDGEMENTS

The author would like to thank the Saskatchewan Arts Board for financial support provided while this book was being written. Thanks are also due to Don MacKay for his thoughtful reading and invaluable advice on the manuscript. The manuscript was started and received its final polish at the Saskatchewan Writers and Artists Colony, a program of the Saskatchewan Writers Guild. Members of Notes from the Undergound and the Poets Combine provided helpful suggestions on several poems.

Staffs of several institutions were helpful in locating the photographs which are reproduced here with their permission. The cover photograph is a detail from *Steerage Deck of the SS Pennland, 1883*, in the City of New York's Byron collection. *The Deck of SS Amsterdam* by Frances Benjamin Johnston, 1910, the photograph of female immigrants undergoing eye examination at Ellis Island, 1911, and Liberty Head, are from the collection of the Library of Congress. William Notman's photograph of Sitting Bull and Buffalo Bill is from the collection of the McCord Museum of Canadian History in Montreal. The picture of Sitting Bull is actually a detail of the same photo. *Singhalese Woman Awaiting Deportation* is from the Keystone-Mast Collection of the University of California Museum of Photography. All the stereoscopic images are from the collection of the author.

The excerpts from the haunting song, "The Young Heir" which appear in "Grave of John Rice," are used by permission of Margaret Bennett, who collected the song and translated it from the Gaelic. The song appears on her CD, *in the sunny long ago*...which is produced by Tartan Tapes (footstomping@tartantapes.com) of Edinburgh, Scotland.

Poems included in this manuscript received *Grain Magazine's* Anne Szumigalski Award in 2002. The award was provided for the best poem or sequence of poems published in Grain during the year. An early version of this manuscript received an honourable mention for the Saskatchewan Writers Guild's John V. Hicks Award. Other poems were broadcast on CBC Saskatchewan's Gallery and appeared on-line in Redneck. Excerpts from the two sequences, *Madmen I Have Known* and *Illustrated Statue of Liberty* were adapted and performed at Globe Theatre's On the Line series in 2001 and 2002.

About the Author

Bruce Rice has published two previous volumes of poetry – *Daniel*, which received the 1989 Canadian Authors Association Award, and *Descent Into Lima*. His work has appeared on CBC Radio and in such magazines as *Grain, Fiddlehead, Canadian Author and Bookman, Prairie Fire, Event, NeWest Review, Fiddlehead,* and *RedNeck*. It has been anthologized in *100% Cracked Wheat, 200% Cracked Wheat, 2000% Cracked Wheat, Heading Out: the New Saskatchewan Poets, Open Windows, Lodestone, Beyond Borders* and *Facing the Lion*. Bruce lives and works in Regina.

His work has been adapted for many performances. Poems in *The Illustrated Statue of Liberty* recieved *Grain Magazine's* 2002 Anne Szumigalski Award, an editor's chair award for the best poem or sequence appearing in *Grain* during the year.